HEY DOC!

THE BATTLE OF OKINAWA AS REMEMBERED BY
A MARINE CORPSMAN

ED WELLS

Edited by
SHANNON D. WELLS

PEARL HANDLE PRESS

CONTENTS

FOREWORD

Around ten years ago, I was given the handwritten pages that became this book. My Grandmother had carefully written out what my Granddaddy told her over several days in her perfect script.

The stories weren't quite in chronological order, and some parts seemed disconnected. I typed them up and arranged them as best I could. A year ago, after Granddaddy passed, I took another look at what we'd put together and decided to take another run at it.

Granddaddy spoke little of the War until the last 10 or so years of his life, and then it was a common subject. Even with all his references to it, there were still stories I had never heard in this manuscript, ones that I'm sure Grandmother had never heard either.

This is my best effort at putting his words in a

proper order and context. All the words are his own. I have only arranged and re-arranged, and added a few words for clarity when I had to.

As I write this note, it's 4th of July weekend, and there's an American flag in my front yard. I remember the sacrifice Granddaddy and others like him made and continue to make. I hope this book reminds and educates others as well.

-Shannon D. Wells, Editor

*Please consider leaving a short review. It helps others decide if they're interested. Thanks!

1

INTRODUCTION

Why have I undertaken this story of my Okinawa experiences? My job placed me all over the country and enabled me to get the big picture. I have written about the things I saw. Everyone else except Sledge and Manchester use second hand information.

Neither of them reported from the viewpoint of corpsman. This material could only be written by me. There is no fiction in my story. I witnessed everything recorded herein.

Combat is a combination of noise, dirt, smoke and steel. Vision is impaired by blue, yellow, brown and white smoke. The impact of scrap iron and bullets to the body is relatively quiet. A few strikes do cause a cry or exclamation, but most do not. The shock that accompanies cut short most verbal responses.

Some wounds cause paralysis at the time of impact. Some others cause loud and continual outcries. These are very painful for their companions to have to endure.

Requests to "shut up" were frequently heard. Seriously injured people called for their mothers. I usually told them their mother would arrive soon. This was lying but it brought comfort to a dying person. There was no hospice service available. All officers and 255 enlisted men of our original strength were killed (130) or wounded except for 5. How they were untouched is a complete mystery.

I have a personal idea that heaven needed a change of the guard and selected 130 of "B" Company 4th regiment for the prestigious honor. I will defend this opinion until I see differently. I expect to see them again and hear a greeting of "Hey Doc, all have been waiting for you." We paid an incalculable price for this victory. All were fighting for mankind's freedom as well as America's.

Some of the events related here are very plain in my memory. Others are incomplete. I remember what happened but do not remember when or where. I believe these blanks are caused by my mind trying to protect me from events that are so extreme that they are unacceptable.

I never expected to be killed and kept a vision of survival constantly in sight. I may have forgotten to smile at all times to demonstrate my reputation as "Smiley Wells"!

I did make a conscious effort to be cheerful and optimistic. I felt that the troops were giving their everything for us. Corpsmen were covered by their blood which would wash clean but nothing would replace their lives or limbs. I had several holes in my trousers and jacket but I have no idea when they happened. I am of the opinion that my guardian angel had been very busy. I was being protected.

To think about this battle sixty-one years later, I have this synopsis. I would not take a million dollars for the memories or ten cents to have to repeat them. You can consider yourself made of good material if you were not traumatized by the events you had been through. These events prepared you to face civilian life eagerly. Nothing could be as difficult as war.

Can the world endure another conflagration of this proportion? Perhaps diplomats will thrive where war has already failed to enable the world's populations to settle disagreements. The lives of my great-grandchildren will depend upon this becoming a reality. Wars are started by old men and carried out by young men.

The Okinawa people were the greatest losers in this battle. They suffered more than 15,000 casualties. Their entire heritage was blown up. Their land was desecrated by both America and the Japanese. The destruction of their property was almost total.

We met old men and women and children. There were no young people. If they wanted to go into a combat area, they just wandered in. They made no effort to avoid the war around them. Animal life consisted of a few skinny horses, goats, and dogs.

All casualty figures in my story are taken from the History of the Sixth Marine Division compiled by the U.S. Marine Corps. All of the events are my own memories. I believe my memory is as reliable as any one else's. This was how things happened from my fox hole. Wars differ from hole to hole, just as everything is seen differently by each individual in life.

My overall purpose in writing this story was to provide a true report of the hospital corpsmen in combat. I did not intend to glamorize the corpsman, but to show their purpose as reinforcement to the Marine in combat. I never met a Marine that I did not admire and respect. Marines are the best fighting men in the armed forces.

War is the most exhilarating human emotion, excluding the problem of avoiding death, which is always nearby to take the careless or those who made unwise choices.

2

BEFORE THE WAR

I was able to go to college one year. I was drafted three days after my eighteenth birthday.

At the Selective Service evaluation, the person doing the interviewing said, "You have had chemistry and would make a good medic. We need corpsmen. Go over and get in line for the Navy."

I moved rapidly from Navy boot camp to hospital corps school to Marine Corps Medical School to assignment to "B" Company of the 6th Battalion of the 4th Regiment as Senior Corpsmen.

This occurred in a less than one year. I was now on Guadalcanal in training for the next campaign. This was five months of vigorous preparation for actual combat.

During this training school for combat, there was somewhat more free time than in the usual schools.

There was a shortage of barbers. Someone had a pair of clippers, a comb, and a pair of scissors. I was asked if I could use them. I said that I would try.

I became the after hours, free-of-charge barber. I also trimmed toenails and gave massages. I was available for almost any request for assistance.

I take this occasion to say that our Company Commander, Mr. James, was the greatest Marine that I ever met! Baker Company was most fortunate to be under his leadership. Captain Charley James was the greatest Marine I ever met. A most admirable man. To my knowledge, he has left no descendants, a loss to mankind.

I never doubted that he could walk on water while singing "Danny Boy". Mr. James had been born in England in 1902. He immigrated to American at age twelve. He joined the Marines at age eighteen and had remained in the corps.

He was notorious throughout the Marines Corps for having managed the rifle range at Quantico. This is the major Marine base at Quantico, Virginia. There he was known as Gunner James. He was now Captain James. His most used command was, "I am going to be on you like an angry God on a Jew peddler," when someone did something to displease him.

Mr. James did not use profanity. One day, I

asked him the meaning of this phrase. He very patiently explained that I should look into the Bible at the things that happened to Joseph's brothers after they sold him to the slave traders who were going to Egypt.

I did and discovered that his brothers suffered the following: their sheep and goats had scabies, a terrible hail rained down on them, bandits attacked their families and lastly there was a famine in their land! I got the idea that they had experienced a terrible series of unpleasantness.

The 4th Regiment had another protector in a Catholic priest named Father Redmond.

He always went with us into combat. He was the most influential person in the Pacific theater of war. The Admirals King, Nimitz, and Halsey were officially in charge, but unofficially Father Redmond was in charge.

On our trip to Okinawa, I happened to be on the same LST as Father Redmond. I was fortunate to hear several of his sermons. They were inspiring, stronger than horseradish, and sobering.

Father Redmond was the final authority on anything to do with the troop's welfare. He would do anything to help a Marine and frequently did so. He was absolutely devoted to our Marines. In troops welfare matters, he could do anything that needed to be done. He had power and influence.

One day in Okinawa we were having a rest day. I heard some gunfire to our right rear. There was also some loud conversation about 200 yards down the hill. We learned that the loud conversation was coming from Father Redmond and his Jeep driver. They had taken cover in a cave on the road to an army unit on our left. They had a large white bundle, which they had made by tying the four corners of a sheet together.

Father Redmond said that the bundle was full of donuts that he was bringing to us. He thought that we were firing on him. He took the strongest objection to this situation and wanted it stopped NOW!

What was really happening was that a cave on our left had been overlooked somehow in the previous battle. Some Japs were in it and popped out every few minutes and took shots at the Padre. As soon as Mr. James saw what was going on, he told Vana to take his squad closer to the cave and send the Japs to their emperor. After a few shots and some WP grenades, silence returned to the area.

Father Redmond got back into his Jeep along with his driver. They disappeared in a cloud of dust. We assumed his feelings were hurt. We never received our donuts!

Another Father Redmond story...in the invasion of Guam the enemy gave us a very vigorous reception by artillery. Guam has about one half mile of shallow water where we landed. These artillery shells hit one LCVP and landed near a couple of others, turning them over. This damage resulted in several being wounded and some killed. The wounded and the dead were brought to the shore and placed in a row for appropriate disposition.

Father Redmond started giving the final rites to the dead. He came to a Marine named Breen. He began the final rites for Breen. The service was interrupted by PFC Breen getting up, pulling on his backpack, picking up his rifle, and going to his platoon. The story went around that Father Redmond had raised him from the dead! I did not see this, but was told this by several witnesses.

3

CORPSMEN

Why are Navy hospital corpsmen placed in the Marine Corps? They are there to bring health and medical care to the troops. Enlisted men get a three month special school in field medical techniques. Most corpsmen have worked at a hospital facility as well.

A Marine Rifle Company of 250 has seven corpsmen in its ranks. Their skills run from amputations and blood transfusions to routine immunizations. These seven are supervised by a senior corpsman.

I was "B" Company senior corpsman. The corpsmen lived with the company and participated in all training exercises. This promoted camaraderie and bonding between the corpsmen and their sphere of responsibility.

I never told a wounded fellow that he would die or be crippled. Those who were very seriously wounded, life threatening, usually seemed to ask for their mother. Very few of the patients ever asked for their father. These fellows usually expired within a few minutes. I always assured my patients that they would soon be in a hospital being cared for by a hospital nurse and would soon return to duty with their friends.

On the occasion when death was obviously a matter of seconds or minutes, I would just hold the hands of those who desired that comfort. I felt I was making a difference by doing anything that seemed to be desired or helpful. In summary, corpsmen were replacements for doctors, mothers, fathers and clergymen and gave services that were very much appreciated.

I didn't feel that I was invincible, but rather protected, with an assurance that I was safe. This was a source of comfort to me when there was no place to hide and my fate was being decided by unknown forces, unapproachable and final.

I will explain later in this story how I was appointed to serve "B" Company as gunnery sergeant. I suspect I was the only senior corpsman to have dual duty.

The supply section of the Marine Corps was

dependable most of the time. The most important supplies were food, water, bullets, and mail. Mortar ammunition was unavailable a couple of times because the enemy blew our ammunition ships up.

On Guadalcanal, we had no meat or vegetables for three months because of Navy ship problems. We survived on dehydrated eggs and potatoes and bread. The Company had a black jaguar as Company mascot. He learned to eat our food. The mail allowed us to hear from home while we were waiting for assignment.

Friendships between team members were life-long commitments. I still receive mail and phone calls from former associates after sixty years.

I recently received a call complaining that my medical service had been too good by causing him to be returned to duty sooner than he wanted. I saw General Friberg at a Marine reunion. He said that I had been excessively slow on checking on him. I had taken forty years.

Modern combat functions as a group of teams. All parts of the team function as an infantry rifle company. We usually operated with Able Company on our left, Charlie Company on our right.

Most military assignments are by company. The company commander made the final assignments to be carried out by individual fire teams. Control passes down to the individual member in a structured manner.

No one decides to start fighting independently. Seargent York in WWI was an exception. Even he was indirectly obeying instructions on enabling the rest of his company to move forward.

World War II began when the Japanese government made a decision that their armed forces superior attitude could cause the other occupants of the planet to yield to their desires. Big mistake. Their superiority did not convince America. The Japanese finally surrendered when they realized that America would defeat them militarily if they continued the war.

The atomic bomb was the final weapon that showed them that to continue the war would bring total destruction to their nation. America's greatest loss was the lives of the young men in our military forces. This was incalculable to America and the world.

4

OKINAWA STARTS

The Battle for Okinawa started at 8:00 AM on April 1, 1945 with the order to "land the landing force." Okinawa looked very similar to the other islands in the Pacific. This view was soon changed. Our Navy was covering it with everything they had that would explode. Company B or Baker Company had one casualty at our landing site.

A short Naval gunfire shell put a piece of steel into the shoulder of one of our Marines. He was evacuated to the rear, never to return. We moved inland a couple of miles without any opposition until just before sundown.

Dark occurred almost without a pause from full brightness of day to absolute darkness. Baker Company collided with an unknown size enemy force. The fire fight lasted about five minutes as darkness suddenly descended on us.

We had one casualty. An enemy machine gun fire hit one of our Marines on the top of his head. If he had been one inch shorter, he would have been injury free. The Marine's name was Peterson.

This wound was life-threatening. I got on the radio and requested an ambulance immediately to evacuate Peterson to the rear for the needed surgery.

The person I was talking to came back with the opinion that I was insane to make such a request for the following reasons: darkness, unfamiliarity with the route, and fear of being shot by our Marines. I would have to care for him overnight until an ambulance could be sent.

The area that we were told to "dig in for the night" was solid rock and totally resistant to our entrenching tools. Nearby was a dead horse still hitched to a two-wheeled rice cart, which was overturned and had spilled about thirty bags of rice. I made a circle of the rice bags and began giving Peterson a blood transfusion.

I continued giving him blood until he was evacuated the following day. About 2:00 AM, when I was checking the needle in his arm, a nausea attack caused him to vomit in my face. His last meal had been beans and wieners. This was my baptismal on Okinawa.

The ambulance arrived at daybreak and started Peterson on his evacuation journey. We received a letter from him in a few weeks. He was in Philadelphia Naval Hospital. He had gone dancing with his wife and was doing well.

The previous day's battle was resumed and continued all day. Those of us who were "green troops" soon became veterans. We were hit with the complete enemy inventory of ammunition, rifles, machine guns and mortar fire.

We had our company commander, three platoon officers, and several of our enlisted men killed on this second day. There were many wounded including another platoon officer. We did have success in battle.

An East Texas rifleman named Durisoe, re-enacted Sergeant York's famous scene in World War I. Durisoe gobbled like a turkey and one at a time five Japanese officers let their curiosity cause them to stick their heads over this ridge. We were fighting from the west side of a ridge about fifty feet high and fifty feet wide. The top was "knife like" forcing anyone wishing to walk on it to do so in a crosswise manner.

Durisoe had picked these five enemy officers at the bottom of the ridge on the east side. When I came along, the Marines in the area were attempting to get someone to go get the Japanese officers swords and pistols. A pot of one hundred dollars had been raised for the taker. This was a very dangerous proposal as there was an unknown number of the enemy still occupying the area. There were no takers for this proposal.

Someone looking through binoculars spotted an enemy mortar crew starting to set up an eighty-one mm mortar on this ridge further north. Rifleman Durisoe put his rifle up and fired one shot. The leader of the mortar crew fell dead causing the rest of the crew to disappear rapidly into the brush further east. Apparently they did so because they couldn't hear the shot or see Rifleman Durisoe.

When we got to this location some two hours later, the mortar crew leader was laying surrounded by his scattered mortar and ammunition. This distance was a minimum of one mile. Rifleman Durisoe had saved us from a horrible blood bath. This extraordinary feat was never recognized by a medal or commendation. This should be corrected now.

This battle ended at darkness when the enemy

disappeared in the night. I imagine that they sent a report to TOJO that, "those Marines do fight!"

The third day was an unopposed stroll, really a march, toward the eastern shore. We dug our foxholes on a trail leading from one unnamed village to another. During the night, three or four shots were heard along with some profanity. When daylight came, one dead enemy was lying near a foxhole occupied by a Marine named Sergeant Barr. He gave his account of what had happened.

Someone came down the trail. He challenged him for the password. He heard nothing. He then shot the person. The fellow had been carrying a sheet bundle of condoms. There seemed to be ten thousand scattered around a ten foot area. In the dead soldier's backpack, was a pornographic plate.

Barr insisted that he had saved him from a life of depravity by killing him. It seemed logical at the time to us. He was likely moving supplies from a house of prostitution to a house that we hadn't overrun.

The fourth day on our eastward journey, we were fired upon by a sniper located in a sugar mill smoke stack. He was silenced promptly.

The following day we walked to the east coast beach. The only notable thing we saw was a number of strange fish. They were white, box-like shaped fish. Years later, I learned their variety to be "trunk" fish. Bombs had blown them out of the bay onto the beach.

On day six, we turned north and started to Nago, the second largest city on the island. We rested here two days before joining in the battle to take the Motobu Peninsula. We were ordered to join the 29th and 22nd regiments to move through this peninsula.

On the morning of April 10th, before the company moved out, standard operating procedures called for a squadron to probe our perimeter to be sure that we were not walking into an ambush. Sergeant Joe Hoit's squadron was selected to check the area. I was asked to accompany them.

We started across a bean field toward the mountains on our north. When we were about two hundred feet from our starting point, the enemy started firing on us with a nambu machine gun.

We all ran to a nearby ditch. The ditch was filled with small trees and large rocks. We felt that we would be safe in this ditch. Bad choice! The enemy was high enough on the mountain to fire into this ditch. He just went down the line firing on us. There were thirteen of us in the ditch. Twelve were wounded or killed.

Sergeant Hoit was the only one who survived unhurt. I received a bullet through the side of my left thigh. I treated the wounded, including myself, as quickly as possible. There was a light fog in the hills above us. We couldn't find the shooter but we fired in any likely appearing place. We called for help. Our Commanding Officer James finally stopped the firing, "Let him have this mountain, we will go on up where we have been told to go."

5

—————

THE SLOG

Rain began in the later part of April and continued through June. Our equipment to protect us in rain was a poncho and a shelter half. When a half was with another, it made a small tent. This was only water resistant, not waterproof.

The temperature ranged from 50-90 degrees. There were no paved roads. Rain produced some of the most extreme muddy roads imaginable. I witnessed four tanks pulling a fifth to extract one that was stuck in a hole. Our trucks had to go through mud to their doors.

When we joined the 29th and 22nd regiments, the enemy was well prepared to resist our plans. They had previously dug a system of trenches connecting the caves. The caves were also well supplied with food, munitions, and an elaborate communication system.

They had artillery equipped to deliver "proximity fused shells" on us. The shells exploded about one hundred feet above the surface and were effective in stopping our progress. This was a new experience for most of us.

The Japanese had a set of large brass binoculars, 15 feet long with a four inch lens mounted on a tripod on top of Mount Yae-Take. They could see what we were doing and where we were. I looked through the binoculars after the battle. I could see in detail where we landed at Nago seven or eight miles away.

The Navy put a great amount of gunfire on the mountain. The Navy Air Force bombed the area with great success. After three days with the Navy's participation and our firing all our guns and finally hand to hand combat we had possession of the peninsula.

The Japanese had blown up the only bridge to cross the forty to fifty foot deep canyon. There was one road around the peninsula. We had to carry our food and supplies down the side of the canyon wall and up the other side. The ambulances, trucks, and tanks could only go that far due to the depth of the canyon.

There were thirty-five to forty "suicide" wood boats out in the harbor. They were approximately twenty feet long and carried five hundred pounds of explosive. Their planned purpose was to run them into our ships with the driver jumping out at the last minute when the explosives were ready to detonate.

The boats were manned by Koreans wearing light blue uniforms. The Japanese wore olive color uniforms with short pants and leggings. The Naval Air Force bombed them and blew them out of the water onto the beach causing them to explode. We licked our wounds for a couple of days.

We were then ordered to go to the extreme north end of the island. We all made the trip of forty-two miles in one day. The commanding officer told us that this was a "world record." Everything that we owned was in our backpacks so that seemed like a long walk!

On this march, we flushed out a few enemy soldiers, one a very embarrassed one. He appeared about one hundred yards uphill in sparse small trees about head high. The A and C companies were with us. The entire battalion started firing at him. He finally disappeared over the hill a half mile ahead.

We had witnessed another unexplainable event four days earlier on Motobu. From the top of the tallest hill, we observed fifty-seven Navy planes take off from a carrier and attempt to bomb this island off Sesoko. All of the planes missed the island from a height of one thousand feet with no one firing at them. We couldn't help but wonder how they graduated from bombardier school!

About 10:00 AM, our radio man received the message of the death of President Franklin Roosevelt. We were all saddened with this news. A few minutes later, the news came of the death of the reporter Ernie Pyle.

6

SUGAR LOAF

Other writers have concluded that the battle for Sugar Loaf was the most costly battle in the war.

I cannot report the details of that terrible night. I do remember that I was very busy but the details are unavailable. I did conclude that there was not enough space on that mound to bury all the dead.

We had been on the north end of Okinawa when we were given orders to go south to join the battle for Sugar Loaf Hill.

As we came near the conflict, we started receiving sporadic fire of a terrible sounding projectile, which we named a "screaming meemie." In the air, it looked like two barrels welded together with an added tail-fin, totaling about twelve feet in length and thirty-six inches in diameter.

The impact that it made was a hole large enough to bury a house. The hole was eight to ten feet deep and twenty feet in diameter. We took azimuths on their launching places and approximate distances. We reported them to headquarters to have them bombed and placed under Naval gunfire from the Tennessee, a battleship lying off the coast.

There was a group of men from the battleship who controlled the firing and were with us most of the time. The group, an officer and five or six men, was called the "Joint Assault Signal Company" or "Jasco." They conversed with the gunners on the ships telling them when and where to fire.

The Japanese firing the "screaming meemies" were never found or slowed down. Later, one of the launch sites was found. It was in a cave and on rails. The ammunition was in a cave too. The Japanese had fully equipped the caves with their ammunition and supplies. Headquarters gave us the following facts to make us feel better when they couldn't do anything about the Japanese firings.

The Japanese had built rails and rolled the launches out on the rails and then fired at us. Rolling the launches back into the caves for reloading took some thirty minutes. So, they couldn't be fired more often than every thirty minutes. This was little comfort to us when we looked at the hole they made as well as having to hear the terrible screaming noise they made.

Two days before the assault on Sugar Loaf Hill, a Marine, James Cochran, came to me and gave me a Navy nurse's cap insignia.

He said, "Doc, I don"t feel good about this campaign. I want you to keep this insignia for me. When I was wounded at Guam, I was sent to Honolulu to recuperate. While there, I met a Navy nurse and we became engaged to be married after this war is over. The cap device is our marriage troth."

This conversation took place about 5:00 PM. The next morning at 8:00 AM an army unit started firing four point two inch mortars having a range of eight miles.

This shell weighed about one hundred pounds and stood about forty-eight inches tall. When the first round was dropped, it made a lot of smoke, not normally coming out of the tube slow. Its upward trip was wobbly indicating a faulty round. When it got to about two hundred feet above the ground, it turned around and headed back to earth.

The impact was within two feet of James Cochran. He was blown into many pieces, leaving one foot in one shoe. I don't know if the graveyard registration gave it a burial.

James was from South Carolina. He continually sang a hillbilly song that went like this "I called and I called but nobody answered." James had been carrying the nurse's insignia for nearly two months on Okinawa when he asked me to be its custodian.

Did he have a premonition of his future? I certainly wondered. I mailed the insignia to the nurse whose name and address were inscribed in the back. I never heard from her. I speculated that there was a "Dear John" letter on it way. He had been too far away for too long.

Later this same day, someone spotted some of the enemy troops moving supplies into their caves. We decided that our tanks could fire directly on them. Our entire tank battalion, now eighteen, came up. We were ordered to accompany them to protect them from enemy foot soldiers, using satchel charges and bazookas. We were obliged to run to keep up.

I saw a 155mm artillery shell coming. When a projectile comes below the horizon or below the brink of another hill, they are plainly visible. The shell exploded one hundred feet ahead of us; a large piece of the shell came buzzing toward us. I looked at Gigilo. His head was lying on the ground in an upright position while his body was still standing up next to it.

I started running. Giglio's body was still standing

when I went over the hill. I have always wondered it was standing when the graveyard registration arrived to give it a burial. His green eyes haunted me for days.

When the tanks got to the desired position, it was 10:00 AM. By 10:30 AM, the last tank was burning. The enemy had destroyed all of them in thirty minutes. They had a 47mm high velocity anti-tank gun that would shoot through the tanks.

While we were looking at the burning tanks, the following occurred. A red Japanese dog came out of a cave and sniffed the air like she was meeting some-one. A couple of minutes later, one of our Marine guard dogs ran up to her. He mounted her and they became connected. When this happened, the war stopped.

Both sides stopped everything. It became absolutely silent. We observers did not understand the armistice. In a few minutes, the dogs separated. The red Japanese female went back into the cave. The Marine guard dog returned to our lines. The war instantly resumed.

This story has been widely reported by other writers. I was impressed to know the enemy was observing us even though we couldn't see them in the caves. Why they stopped the war for ten minutes, I do not have the foggiest notion. Why did our side cease all firing? Weird and unexplainable. I suppose that the "Gods of War" took time out to have a cup of coffee!

My thoughts returned to the tank crews who had seen their entire battalion destroyed in thirty minutes. If any damage had been done to the enemy, it was not apparent. They had been ordered to the wrong place at the wrong time. A horrible waste of good men and material. Shameful by my evaluation.

At 10:30 PM, we were ordered to go up on Sugar Loaf to reinforce the K Company. They were fighting hand to hand and believed they would be overrun without help. The rain was coming down in torrents. Flares were firing continuously. I found a six-foot hole and remained there all night. A dead Japanese lay in the bottom. I tried to cover him with mud.

All the weapons of war were being used by both sides. A red-headed fellow named McGee was hit on his white phosphorus grenade which exploded setting him on fire. He burned all night leaving only his shoes by daybreak.

White phosphorus grenades were carried on the straps on 782 gear or backpacks. Their purpose was to throw them into caves to smoke out the Japanese.

The survivors seemed to have a condition described as "a thousand yard stare." The pupils dilated, but you do not see, just stare. You hear but you do not understand. Reality has leaked out and left you numb. This condition is usually temporary.

Treating the wounded was hectic as soon as daybreak arrived. "Doc we need you over here," was a constant call. I went from one to another as quickly as I could to treat each man.

When we realized that Sugar Loaf was ours, we walked around looking at what was left. We saw the reverse slope for the first time.

At ground level was the entrance to the Japanese hospital, which was in caves. Outside the hospital on the road to Naha, bodies were stacked five deep for a distance of at least one hundred yards. The number was more than a thousand waiting to be buried by someone.

This was the largest number of dead people that I had ever seen. This caused a feeling of awe to think that this group of our enemy was deceased and we were still alive and fighting.

7

AFTER THAT

We were ordered to take a position in some tombs on the way to Shuri Castle. The families laid their deceased on a shelf in the tomb.

After the body was thoroughly decayed, one of the family was given the honor to go into the cave and scrape the bones. The bones would then be placed into a tall vase-like container. The vases would be as tall as forty-eight inches.

We quickly removed these vases. We not only needed the space for our men and supplies but the vases still have a very strong undesirable odor!

Our time in these tombs was a great deal more comfortable than being out in the rain and mud as we had been for weeks. The tombs were dry. After being in wet weather for such an extended time with only a poncho for cover and mud for a mattress, we weren't in very good condition.

When we would take our shoes off, the skin also came off many times. Then, the next layer of skin would bleed. All that we could do was to put on dry socks and wool if possible. Wool was better for our feet in this situation than cotton socks.

The tombs were about thirty-five feet wide and thirty feet deep. They were tall enough for us to stand upright. Our "B" Company was split because there wasn't enough space for all of us even at our low strength of thirty-four. The other group was located about two hundred feet away in other tombs.

The fourth day of our time in the tombs, two unknown generals and General Geiger came to us and asked to see our commanding officer.

I pointed to the tomb where he was and gave them some advice: that it wouldn't be a good idea to go to Mr. James because there was a sniper covering the space between our tombs. He fired at everything crossing that area. We had done everything we could think of to eliminate him but to no avail.

The generals said that they would be all right and proceeded to cross the field. The sniper bounced a few bullets around them. They wisely fell to the ground and started crawling in some tank ruts that were nearby.

Some fifteen minutes later, the generals returned crawling on their elbows. They were now well-covered by mud. I resisted the temptation to tell them "I told you so."

The sniper remained active until we left the area. The generals left the way they came and were happy to be able to leave.

In a few days, we were ordered to take Shuri Castle. This had been the location of their capitol for four hundred years. On Monday, we started, but the Japanese would not give an inch. On Tuesday, we tried again just at daybreak when the sun was on the horizon.

I was called to a foxhole about a hundred feet up the hill we were on. "Williams needs you bad!" I found Williams lying outside his foxhole. He had been "stitched" by a mambo machine gun.

"Stitched" was a term used by Marines when one was hit from the head all through the body. He had fourteen holes in his body with four of them in his chest. I got into his foxhole and gave him morphine and started a blood transfusion.

About half of the blood transfusion was in him when a mortar shell came into the foxhole with us. It missed my head by a few inches and was sticking in the corner of this foxhole. I recognized this shell to be an 81mm size about fifteen inches long and capable of blowing us into small pieces. This caused me great apprehension for my future. My spirit left my body.

I found myself in a brightly lit amphitheater standing in front of a desk. Behind the desk was a Middle-Eastern person, with olive skin about six feet tall, a thin, hooked nose with a white beard that came down to his waist and white hair that came to his waist.

He was sitting on a chair looking at a book on the desk. The book was about twelve by fifteen inches and twelve inches thick. It had a wooden front and back. They pages were bound together by a leather thong.

This person did not speak. He just turned to a page showing my name and pointing to it. He was dressed in a long white robe and had sandals on his feet. Stacked near his right hand was a pile of harps several dozen in number. They appeared to be made of walnut. The harps had about twenty strings. I became aware of a strong desire to have and play one of these instruments.

On the left side, three or four blocks in the distance, people were running in a random manner through flames about five feet tall. There were no sounds coming from this area. These scenes caused me to think that I had been deposited in Hades!

I immediately started screaming as loud as I

could "A horrible mistake has been made! I do not belong here! Check your book again! I am in the wrong place! Look again!" A voice came from somewhere. I did not see anyone. The voice said,"Be quiet, you are not in Hades but in the heavenly place."

The voice told me to enter a tunnel that was in front of me. The tunnel was about ten feet wide and high. There was a continuous assortment of people on this moving sidewalk. They were moving at a speed of seven or eight miles per hour.

I decided to become a passenger. The tunnel was lighted and I could hear the background music. After I had gone a few blocks, I became aware that this tunnel was going to run into a wall but it forked with a branch going both right and left.

My immediate problem was to decide which way I should choose. I decided to take the right tunnel. Just as I approached the wall, I was suddenly someplace entirely different.

I saw the sun as a red ball. It was a ten-degree angle to the horizon. The sun had been just on the horizon when I started to treat Williams.

As I began to become aware of my surrounding, mortars were exploding, small arms fire appeared to be thick enough to walk on. Artillery shells were exploding all around. One struck a tree that was about fifteen inches around, cutting it down and blowing a part of it near me.

My mind told me there was a war going on in this place just like the place where I had been at the start of my day. I had no idea where I was.

Someone called, "Doc Wells, we need you down here!" Upon hearing my name, reality returned. I realized that I was standing in a foxhole with Williams whose body was cold and stiff. I looked at the mortar shell that was still unexploded in the corner of the foxhole.

I quit breathing! I took the needle out of William's arm and threw the remainder of the blood into the weeds. I carefully got out of the foxhole as fast as I could.

I ran down the hill where I had been called. My new patients were a couple of foxhole mates who had failed to disarm a booby trap that they put out for the enemy the previous night. One of them had exploded it while urinating.

This caused serious wounds to them. One was dead and the other in very serious condition. I got him ready and evacuated him to the rear medical station. I had a continuous series of wounded men that day. I reflected on my "Williams" experience.

I decided that I would question his foxhole mate to learn if I had spoken out audibly. This came to naught. When I got back to the area, he had been blown into pieces by another mortar.

We were successful in taking Shuri Castle that day.

I did not normally place myself on the imaginary line called "the front." My job required me to be accessible to the entire company.

A mortar shell landed within thirty feet of me, almost on a Marine named Dickerson. This shell exploded leaving Dickerson's left leg barely attached to his body.

I used my K bar knife to finish removing his leg and got a tourniquet on his stub. I gave him a couple of shots of morphine. He was not conscious.

I could not see anyone in this area so I put him on a "fireman carry" and started toward our rear to find someone to call an ambulance. After walking some one hundred fifty yards, I found help. The medical supply section had sent me a nylon stretcher to evacuate Dickerson. I got it out and we started to the rear with Dickerson. We found the radio operator and I called to be met by an ambulance.

They said that the bridge over the Asa River had been blown up for the fourth time. We would have to bring him to the west bank of the Asa River. That should be about two miles. The river was in flood since we had had five weeks of continuous rain. No one knew how deep the water was so we entered cautiously. The river was nearly one hundred feet wide and came up to my chin.

The jeep was waiting when we arrived on the side. We put Dickerson on board to go to the hospital and we retraced our steps. About thirty days later, we received a letter from Dickerson. He had been sent to the Naval Hospital in Philadelphia, his hometown. He was doing great. He had been fitted with a prosthesis leg and had gone dancing with his girlfriend! A success story!

A couple of days later, I received a call that the battalion surgeon wanted to see me. He told me that he had recommended me for a Silver Star medal for my "Dickerson effort." I had no idea where he got his information.

A couple of weeks later Chief Boudreau came by and told me that the recommendation had been approved at Naval Headquarters in Honolulu. He further said that the Marine Corps Headquarters in Washington, D.C. would almost automatically approve it.

Six years later, I met our Major at the San Diego Naval Hospital. He told me that the Silver Star medal had come for me. He didn't know where I was so he returned it to the Marine Headquarters. I have not received the medal nor any more information. Sometime perhaps.

We were having a day of rest because the army on our right hadn't caught up with us. The Navy would have called this a "rope Sunday." I had been stretching my hammock. The trees had bent when I heard a loud explosion. We all looked toward its source.

We saw Webster flying through the air about fifty feet high. His jacket had fallen off him. I started running toward his flight path as it happened. It seemed a certainty that he would require my attention when he landed. He came down in a pile of bushes about six to eight feet tall. He got up and walked up to me with a few scratches as his only wounds!

I helped him put his jacket on and asked what happened. He said that there was a small cave to his left. When he got closer, he saw a Japanese flag. He entered the cave and jerked the flag causing an explosion that blew him through space like the man at the county fair that is shot out of a cannon. I offered my opinion that he was the luckiest man on the island to have only a few scratches. No Purple Heart came from this trip!

Later, we were on the north side of our assigned territory on Okinawa, when I heard a call "Hey Doc,

Betz has been hit and needs you!" I started up the hill to him as stretcher-bearers were carrying him toward me. I was about one hundred yards from Betz when I started receiving a lot of machine gun fire.

Bullets started going by my head. I mistook them for hornets or wasps. I started slapping at the "wasps" when the Marines who were carrying Betz yelled to me to go back down.

They said, "The Japs firing at you will kill you!" They would bring Betz to me. This seemed like good advice. I reversed my direction instantly. When I got to the bottom of the hill, I saw the stretcher crew had arrived about where I had been. They started receiving the machine gun fire as I had.

Betz jumped off the stretcher and continued running toward me. He arrived before the stretcher carriers!

When I examined his wounds, I found that his leg was almost completely severed at the ankle level. I could turn his foot ninety degrees right or left without any pain to the rest of his leg. I found two forked limbs and immobilized him so that he could be evacuated. I called for an ambulance to come for Betz.

Another walking wounded arrived before the ambulance arrived. He was Platoon Sergeant Maritada. He was a terrific Marine. He had been shot in his genitals several times. I took my "K bar" knife and cut his trousers in the shape of an upside down apron. I then sprinkled him with sulfa drug and put a twelve by twelve inch bandage on him that let him have a sense of privacy. He was evacuated with Betz to the battalion aid station then to a hospital ship then to be flown to Guam or wherever the wounded could be best treated.

Upon our arrival at Shuri Castle, orders were received to embark on a LST for another amphibious landing. We were taken to the Oroku Peninsula. This enabled us to attack our enemy from a ninety-degree side angle. This gave us a temporary advantage of surprise.

The enemy quickly recovered and began giving us a spirited reception. Mortars started falling from the sky like apples on a windy day. The word came down the line that one of the platoon corpsmen had been severely wounded or killed. It was my responsibility to check this out and replace him if there was no one else available or request a replacement.

On my trip to his location, I passed an old house that had long been deserted. As I passed the back door, I suddenly found myself up to my waist in a hole.

I had stepped into a receptacle where the people stored human waste. This was to be used as fertilizer on their garden. This material was a yellow, pudding-like material. The odor was beyond description! It was horribly over-powering!

When I realized what had happened, my first solution was to just lie there and let another mortar shell solve the problem. Then I remembered that graveyard registration would probably not pick my body up for burial unless I got out of the pit.

I decided to be a human again. I climbed out and removed all of my clothing including my shoes. I kept my K bar knife very sharp. I used it to shave my entire body. I got lucky.

I took the steel pot part of my helmet and followed a small ditch until I found a helmet full of muddy water. I got a sock out of my backpack which I used as a washcloth. I them washed my entire body including my shoes. Then I realized that I had no other clothing to wear.

A hazard of my duties required me to change clothing every five days. This was because the dried blood of my patients would rub my body becoming very painful. My company commander, Mr. James, heard of my plight. He gave his runner his last set of clean dungarees to solve my problem.

Gunnery Sergeant Harry Cankins was seriously wounded. I treated him and sent him to the LCVP that was docked, to take him to a hospital ship.

The duties of the gunnery sergeant was to order food, water, and ammunition as well as to keep the company strength report. The strength report was the number of men who were in the company daily. Mr. James appointed me to be the B Company Gunnery Sergeant. This was in addition to my duties as the senior corpsman.

We had two hundred sixty men when we landed on Okinawa. We were down to thirty-two for a couple of weeks. Military Doctrine says that, "a reduction of twenty-five percent made a company ineffective as a fighting unit." This story is horse feathers!

We charged with our thirty-two members holding our assigned area. No one mentioned that we should ask for a rear echelon position. We would all have been ashamed to be replaced. After this campaign was ended a report said that "over twelve thousand men were evacuated from Okinawa for psychological reasons." This report is a complete fabrication in my opinion.

Baker Company had three men with psychological problems. One was a corpsman who had been in the Guam campaign. When the bullets started flying, he lay down on the ground and cried, "I can't take this!" I sent him immediately to the rear headquarters.

The other two should never have been sent into the battle zone. One was a gunnery sergeant who had fought in the Spanish American War and in the Nicaragua Campaign, 1927-32. The other one was a fifty year old man who was emotionally disturbed. They were also evacuated to the rear headquarters.

The battle for the Oroku Peninsula went easier than our previous battle. We were to go onto Oroku with food and water for two days because the space where the boats could load was only about fifty feet wide and could only land one boat at a time.

One boat would bring in water, another food, and a third ammunition. These boats were the LCP"s Landing Craft Vehicular Personnel. The LCVP's brought in the necessary supplies and then took the wounded out to a hospital ship or to an aid station.

On the second day, Corporal James Eagleton, a BAR man from Tulsa was wounded. I treated him and sent him to the waiting LCVP that was docked.

The third day we were marching through a small valley about one half mile long. A group of Japanese jumped out of spider holes and began firing at our backs.

"Spider holes" are round holes dug large enough for one person. A woven stick top was made to cover the hole. It was then covered with dirt. They were absolutely undetectable.

They were dug near a road or trail, near enough to hear passers-bye. They then would push the covers off and start shooting at us. We took appropriate action to neutralize them.

That night we dug in at the base of a steep hill. Our front line was on the side of this hill. Around ten o'clock that night, a Marine who was dug in about fifty feet up a slope began screaming "Help me! This SOB is trying to stick me with a knife that he has attached to the end of a pole! My gun is jammed!"

This was a bright moonlit night. All of the company could see what was happening. The enemy was chasing him around in his foxhole. The man's name was Masezko. He was jumping all around dodging the knife thrusts. The enemy got too close. Masezko got his hands on his neck and disposed of his problem.

A couple of hours later I was on watch. I spotted a Japanese coming toward my foxhole. He was about one hundred yards away. We had flare illumination about half of the time. The moon was now over the hill. The enemy was running when the light was out and then stopped when the flare came on.

He was moving about forty feet each dark cycle.

I decided that I was going to have to kill him as he came closer to my foxhole. I decided that I must shoot him at the next light cycle. He would be about fifty feet away. I started squeezing the trigger.

A shot rang out nearby. The enemy dropped dead. I breathed a prayer of thanksgiving and let the hammer down on my pistol. I had cottonmouth from the slow approach of the enemy. When morning came I removed a Buddhist prayer wheel from around his neck. Buddha had failed to protect him.

Later that day some of our people on the line sent word to Mr. James to come and witness a ritual-istic suicide. Two Japanese Generals performed the procedure with a back up person to remove their heads. This caused a slowdown in the enemy resistance. We had now withdrawn to a rear area actually one mile into the rear.

We were ordered to dig in when we were at a sweet potato field under the muzzles of our 155 mm artillery guns. Sleeping was almost impossible because they were firing almost continuously over our heads.

We received word that we would be leaving for Guam in two days. On our last day, we were ordered to take a newly arrived Colonel on a mission to give him some combat experience. This was to be a search and destroy mission to the extreme south end of Okinawa.

Mr. James said, "Doc, you've been a good man. I'm going to let you choose who goes. You pick about thirty men. This will be the last combat on this island." I chose 28 of our best. This Colonel was Senator Strom Thurmond's son-in-law.

We considered him to be a VIP. We wanted to impress him with our abilities. Colonel Bell was very impressive when he arrived. He was wearing a suit of Brooks Brothers dungarees, very shiny boots and an elaborately flared hat with gold braid on its bill. All of this on a six foot two inch body that had been perfectly tanned. In addition he smelled good! In contrast, we had had one shower in one hundred days.

There were still a considerable number of enemy soldiers left in scattered groups, especially at house sites. The further south we got, we started taking sniper fire and finding more Japanese soldiers.

About 11 AM, a Japanese soldier jumped out of a brush pile and began firing at Mr. James and myself. Mr. James was shot in the teeth. The sideways shot had removed six teeth. I shot the Japanese from a distance of 50 feet.

I gave Mr. James a battle dressing to bite down on and suggested he return to the base camp for further medical treatment that he needed. We never saw him again.

A new mood came over our group. We changed from a desire to be military sharp to one of revenge. We had regarded Mr. James as untouchable and invincible. We went another mile south and stopped for lunch. We then moved across a two hundred yard bean field that was bounded by an escarpment of rocks and trees on its southern edge. This escarpment rose about fifteen feet to a grassy plain. We started receiving sporadic rifle fire.

One of our more experienced Marines climbed the rocks and looked through a notch. He said, "I see the SOB, Chick you take the low side and I will take the top side. We will get this SOB!"

This Marine was Ed Dunham. He was a very popular and charismatic member of our B Company. Ed raised his head to take another look. A shot was heard. Ed Dunham fell dead at my feet. He had a bullet exactly in the center of his forehead.

Baker Company cried, all of us. We realized that Ed's life had been taken just hours before we would be leaving Okinawa. We were overwhelmed. We further felt that we had paid a terrible price to give a newly arrived Colonel some combat experience. He individually was not responsible, as we were at war.

The enemy was still determined to kill anyone that he could. We had the very same goal.

This was our final death on Okinawa. Someone had a machete and cut a couple of poles. The addition of a shelter-half formed a stretcher to carry Dunham's body to meet the ambulance that I had called to meet us. We carried him across the bean field and the ambulance was waiting for us.

The ambulance took Ed to the cemetery and Colonel Bell back to the base camp.

Four Marine tanks started up the escarpment. I assumed that they were flame tanks on a cave burning assignment. The lead tank had a bulldozer blade on it. He was making a road for the other 3 tanks.

When the second tank entered the escarpment, a Japanese soldier with a backpack on jumped off of a rock onto the tank and exploded the backpack. The explosion blew the turret off of the tank, killing himself, the driver and wounding the other crew members.

The Japanese soldier was blown into 2 pieces. The left leg seemed to go up 200 feet. The rest of the body went up about 80 feet. The remaining tanks went on up the escarpment and over it to complete their assignment. This caused our bitter cup to overflow.

Our thoughts were now directed to return to our base camp and leave Okinawa for Guam. We had lost Mr. James and Ed Dunham on our last day. A heart-breaking day.

We had suffered 400 wounded and 135 killed in the previous 100 days from our B Company. I had given between 45 and 50 blood transfusions, one leg amputation, and applied enough bandages to create several mummies. The following day was July 10, 1945. We boarded a LST at 9 o'clock in the morning returning to Guam.

OCCUPATION

I found a lifeboat on the top deck, got in it and went to sleep. I slept for 7 days seldom awakening to eat. I didn't desire food, only sleep. After seven days of hibernation, I awoke and began to live again. I reflected on what had happened. I recalled the Lord's Prayer. I felt that we had been "through the valley of the shadow of death." God had protected us.

I was thankful that I had been associated with these terrific men and that combat was over for a while. As I reflected on my recent past, I started visiting our survivors who were congratulating each other on their survival. A rifleman whom I did not know came up to me and asked me if I knew my nickname among the troops. I confessed that I didn't know that I had one.

He said I was named as "Smiley Wells." I was overwhelmed by this title.

My cup ran over to think that I could be in this hell on earth for one hundred and one days and be known as Smiley Wells!

I had been given several other things while the battles were in progress; one was a 38 pistol from Potter. Another gift was a silver tea set and then a set of surgical instruments out of the Japanese hospital in the caves on Sugar Loaf, to name a few.

This was almost too much for my 20 year old mind to comprehend. The song "Lord, you have been so good to me," was the best that I could think.

It had taken us six weeks to go from Guadalcanal to Okinawa. We had returned to Guam in less than two weeks. The trip was uneventful. Guam was a very peaceful green island. The weather was warm but a really nice place overall.

We started building our camp. Before we were finished we were ordered to go to the Quartermaster and draw new clothing and helmet covers. We were then ordered to pack for our next destination, Japan.

We were very apprehensive about this trip. We had always been led to believe that we would be invading the Japanese homeland and have our ulti-mate bloodbath. We boarded an LST and departed at 7 mph.

Approximately a week later, we were in the area of the island of Ulithi. It was a very small island with a good harbor. The Navy kept supply ships of food and ammunition there. The ships going to Guam, Saipan, Guadalcanal or any of the islands could stop by for their necessary supplies. There were several ships in the area where we were sailing going to Japan.

The ships started firing their anti-aircraft guns and turning their floodlights toward the sky. We couldn't imagine why all the revelry.

The radiomen picked up the news that Japan had surrendered! We now knew the reason for the fireworks! The radiomen soon received the information that a new type of bomb had been dropped on Japan.

The atomic bomb, termed Little Man was the first atomic bomb dropped, August 6, 1945. We all felt that we could relax somewhat, knowing that we wouldn't be in combat when we arrived in Japan!

The 4th Marines were chosen to go to Yokosuka, Japan to begin the occupation of Japan. This was considered to be an honor because the 4th Marines had been guarding our embassy in Tesing China. They were withdrawn and sent to Corregidor to aid General McArthur in the Philippines. When Corregidor fell, those remaining were captured.

They remained prisoners of the Japanese until the end of the war.

We arrived at the Yokosuka Naval Base the day before the peace treaty was signed. We were at anchor about a mile and a half from the battleship Missouri. The peace treaty ceremony was on the Missouri. The Missouri was the designated site because President Harry Truman was from Missouri. We were fortunate to have the opportunity to view the signing of the peace treaty through binoculars.

We later got onto LCVP's to make the five mile trip to Yokosuka Naval Base where we were to be quartered. The American occupation had begun. The Japanese people were a complete surprise to what we had been expecting. Our former enemies were now our friends.

While we were standing in line awaiting our housing assignments, a black 1929 Cadillac limousine drove by us. A uniformed officer was driving the limousine. There were three Japanese men in evening dress complete with top hats as passengers. These were three of the men who had signed the peace treaty. They were now returning to Tokyo.

The first day that we were ashore we were given liberty. Four of us decided to go to Tokyo. When we arrived in downtown Tokyo, the train stopped at a central station and we disembarked. The scene was indescribable. To the south and west was total destruction; mile after mile of burned out buildings and homes could be seen. To our north and west there wasn't any war damage!

The emperor's residence was in this direction. The bombing had avoided the area of his residence by a mile in all directions. It was as if a line had been drawn around this area and everything outside of the line was obliterated.

The downtown business district was near the emperor's home, so it was intact. The department stores and other businesses were doing business as usual, as if there had not been a war going on.

General McArthur's headquarters had been established in the Imperial Hotel. The MP's had not had time to get the area blocked off. We visited the hotel without a problem. We asked where the General's office was and were told, "On the 2nd floor." We walked by, but he wasn't in his office.

The Japanese populace didn't acknowledge us when we were downtown. We seemed to be invisible to them. They were neither friendly nor were they unfriendly. They just ignored us, probably hoping that we would go away. We boarded the train and returned to base, having mixed emotions about our trip to Tokyo.

9

———

AFTER THE WAR

I was assigned to sick call duty in our medical facility. The duty involved mostly treating minor complaints such as fungus, cuts and blisters. My introduction to the Japanese relationship between doctor and patient, unorthodox to us, came quite soon.

A Japanese fellow working for the occupation forces was accidentally knocked down by a truck. Prudent practice indicated that he should be x-rayed for the possibility of broken bones. We had an arrangement for this to be done at a local hospital. I went with the ambulance to the hospital.

When we arrived the patient was taken to the x-ray department. The technician situated the fellow to be x-rayed. He may have moved an inch or maybe not, but the technician didn't like the position of the patient so she slapped him vigorously.

The Marine ambulance driver grabbed a handful of her uniform and gave her a shaking. He was shoved out of the way and given some "free advice" by the driver. I supposed this to be the first battle of the occupation. It was later explained to us that this "brutal action" to us, was the normal doctor to patient relationship at that time. I feel certain that this behavior no longer exists in Japan between the doctor and patient.

In early October, a very strong typhoon formed in the Pacific. When it reached us in Yokosuka, the winds were very strong and the rain was very heavy. On this day, I was doing my laundry in a machine shop near my quarters. I had found a large pot and some sticks and built a fire to heat the water. I put my clothes in the pot. When I was satisfied that the clothes were clean I put out the fire and started to my quarters.

I saw a broken pole that had fallen to the ground. It had a large number of wires attached to it. I assumed them to be telegraph wires. They were too tall to step over so I grabbed hold of the tallest wire to hold it down so that I could step over the other wires.

This turned out to be a 90 volt direct-current

(the normal voltage for domestic power in Japan) line! I started screaming for help. I then realized no one could hear me above the noise of the storm. I would have to free my hand myself.

My laundry was in my helmet. In my right hand I had a punch stick, a stick that I had used to agitate the clothing. I got the punch stick into my left hand that had seized the wire. I finally pried it open enough to break contact with the current.

I had a great feeling of relief to be released from the hot wires! I was thankful that I happened to have on wooden shower shoes. That kept me from being grounded when I was holding onto the 90 voltage wire! Danger does exist in everyday life, as this event proved to me. My guardian angel was kept busy!

On October 25, 1945, I was given my orders to return to the States! We boarded an LST which took us to Guam. We then boarded another LST which took us to Honolulu. We arrived in Honolulu the week of Christmas.

There was one piece of Christmas decoration in Honolulu. It was a green Christmas rope stretched in a downtown park, about 40 feet in length.

JD Rush, a fellow corpsman, and I met in Honolulu. We had attended corps school together in San Diego. He had been with the 22nd Marines. We were excited to see that each other had made it through the war and were on our way home! In a few days we were sent to a carrier to go to San Diego and home.

10

EPILOGUE

EPILOGUE

This story was written in 2006, sixty years after it occurred. Most of the people are deceased. This is a true report of events that occurred just as written. They are almost all in chronological order from the beginning to the end of the battle for Okinawa.

My life as a civilian has been much less exciting. I have served as Chairman of the Selective Service Board of Creek County, Oklahoma. I served on the Sapulpa City Commission from 1966-1976. I was the Mayor of the City of Sapulpa in 1975-1976.

I am the proud father of two sons and one daughter, the joys of my life. We have four grandchildren and five great-grandchildren. I retired in 1992 after 37 years as a furniture retailer. Earlene and I have been happily married since January 1, 1948.

*Please consider leaving a short review. It helps others decide if they're interested. Thanks!

11

OBITUARY

August 22, 1925 - January 30, 2016

Ed Wells, 90, of Sapulpa, OK died peacefully on Saturday, January 30th, 2016 at Muskogee VA Center, Muskogee, OK.

Ed is survived by his wife, Earlene Wells, of 68

years; his children, sons Waldon and Allen and daughter Karen; daughter-in-law, Anna and son-in-law, William; sisters, Donnie and Nita; brother-in-law, Dick; grandchildren, Nicole (John), Aloyshia (Geary), Sean (Deborah), Shannon (Scott); great-grandchildren, Cole, Samantha, Stephen, Carson, Jackson, Samuel, Solomon, and Rosemarie. Ed also had many nieces and nephews who loved him dearly.

Ed was born on August 22nd, 1925 in Hannah, Oklahoma to Harvey and Beulah Wells. After marrying his beautiful wife Earlene, they moved to Sapulpa, OK where a lifetime of work and family memories began.

Ed served as Chairman of the Selective Services Board of Creek County, Sapulpa City Commission 1966-1976 and Mayor of Sapulpa, 1975-1976. He and Earlene owned and operated Wells Furniture for many years. After Wells Furniture burned down in 1981 he purchased the now-historic Wells Building in downtown Sapulpa. Ed and Earlene owned and operated the Wells Building until their retirement.

One of Ed's proudest accomplishments was serving his country in the Navy in WWII. Ed served as a US Navy hospital corpsman during WWII and as a US Naval commissioned lined officer during his active service in the Korean War. For his bravery, medical treatment he provided to wounded soldiers and the injuries he sustained, he was one of the elite soldiers that received a Purple Heart and the Bronze-star.

In 2006 Ed wrote a book titled "Hey Doc" that told of his time at war during the battle of Okinawa. He served with pride. Above all achievements in Ed's life it was his family that made him the most proud as wrote in the epilogue of his book "Hey Doc."

Ed was an accomplished craftsman and could often be found working with rocks and minerals and sculpting artwork. Many family members and friends are blessed to have received pieces of his artwork.

Ed's home resembled a historical museum. There were books, artwork, figurines, pieces of precious rocks and minerals and statues. For his grandchildren and great grandchildren it was a place of love, knowledge, and stories from his world travels and vast experiences in life.

Ed was a generous man who always helped others when in need. His solid Christian faith was a virtue that never left his side. Our world is a better world to have had him in it for 90 years. His stories will be repeated and his memory will be honored.

His accomplishments will be shared for the rest of our lives. Our hearts are heavy but our souls are at peace now that he is with our Heavenly Father.

His remains are at the Fort Gibson National Cemetery in Fort Gibson, Oklahoma.